REACHING OUT
with a
MESSAGE *of*
HOPE!

REACHING OUT
with a
MESSAGE *of*
HOPE!

WITH SEVEN VITAL KEYS TO EFFECTIVE OUTREACH MINISTRY

CHARLANA KELLY

Pleasant Word
A Division of WINEPRESS PUBLISHING

Pleasant Word (a division of WinePress Publishing, PO Box 428, Enumclaw, WA 98022) functions only as book publisher. As such, the ultimate design, content, editorial accuracy, and views expressed or implied in this work are those of the author.

Unless otherwise indicated, all Scripture quotations are taken from the New King James Version of the Bible, copyright © 1982 by Thomas Nelson, Inc. Used by permission. All rights reserved.

Scripture quotations marked KJV are taken from the King James Version of the Bible.

Scripture quotations marked AMP are taken from the Amplified Bible, Old Testament, copyright © 1965, 1987 by the Zondervan Corporation; the Amplified New Testament, copyright © 1958, 1987 by the Lockman Foundation. Used by permission.

Scripture quotations marked Message are taken from THE MESSAGE: New Testament with Psalms and Proverbs copyright © 1993, 1994, 1995 by Eugene H. Peterson, published by NavPress, PO Box 35001, Colorado Springs, Colorado 80935. Used by permission.

Scripture quotations marked NLT are taken from the Holy Bible, New Living Translation, copyright © 1996. Used by permission of Tyndale House Publishers, Inc., Wheaton, Illinois 60189. All rights reserved.

ISBN 13: 978-1-4141-0919-0
ISBN 10: 1-4141-0919-9
Library of Congress Catalog Card Number: 2006910974

DEDICATION

This book is dedicated to my husband, who for years has encouraged me to go for the dreams and desires God placed in my heart. He has supported me throughout my journey and kept me in balance when I got off the path. He is a great husband, a wonderful friend, and a wise man of God, who loves me beyond reason. For him, I am grateful to God each day! And of course, thank You, Father God, for trusting me with Your message of hope, a poem of love written on the hearts of Your people to a lost generation.

TABLE OF CONTENTS

INTRODUCTION:
A MESSAGE OF HOPE

Not long ago, as I sat in my car at a red light, I noticed that the car in front of me wore a "fish" emblem on its bumper. The moment I noticed it, the still, small voice inside me said, "Not as many people are born again as you think." It was a sobering moment.

We naturally want to believe the best of every person. When we see the markings of Christianity, we assume those who sport them are true followers of Jesus Christ. Not so—more than 82% of Americans say they believe in God[i]; yet only 47% regularly attend worship services in churches across this great nation[ii].

After considering what the Holy Spirit spoke to my heart that day, I remembered what Jesus said in Matthew 7:21–23, "Not everyone who says to Me, 'Lord, Lord,' shall enter the kingdom of heaven, but he who does the will of My Father in heaven. Many will say to Me in that day, 'Lord, Lord, have we not prophesied in Your name, cast out demons in Your name, and done many wonders in Your name?' And then I will declare to them, 'I never knew you; depart from Me, you who practice lawlessness!'"

From that experience came this understanding: Many, even multitudes, who think they know the Lord and call Him by name are far from Him. In other words, not every person with a "fish" emblem on his or her car is God's own. And further, there are many who have never heard the message of salvation through faith in Jesus Christ. The bottom line is that there is still much work to be done, and many laborers are needed to bring in the harvest. Bold witnesses for Christ are being thrust out in every arena to bring glory to God and speak the truth in love to all who have ears to hear. It doesn't matter what our socio-economic status is in this nation, God has positioned a set-apart saint in the right place to bring light and truth in Christ to those who live in darkness.

Chapter 1 ❧

THE MANY FACES OF NEED

God created every individual on the face of this earth. He breathed life into each person's soul. He loved each one so much that He placed an eternal seed within every heart that will cause them to wonder about life after death and eventually choose their eternal destination. Ecclesiastes 3:11 establishes this. God then set us down on earth with a free will to choose our future.

A powerful experience I had with God years ago still haunts me today. I was attending a prayer conference, and during one of the sessions God gave me a vision of a man who was diseased, obviously suffering from starvation, slumped over a rock, and with no life in his eyes. In my mind's eye, he writhed in pain and gasped for every breath.

I realized that the spirit of this man struggled violently within him, for life, but there was none. Immediately I heard this scripture in my heart, "The spirit indeed is willing, but the flesh is weak," (Mark 14:38). The spirit within this man was willing to receive life, even struggling to find it, but his flesh was so sick and hopeless that it was over-powering the spirit within him. Shaken to my very core, I was never the same again. Never again would I look at people as I had, nor would I judge their outward condition. It was forever settled in my heart that the spirit within each person is struggling for life, even when the outward condition seems to have it all together or seems determined to sin and live in destruction. From this experience, I learned not to make any assumptions regarding the salvation of another person.

I now believe that when we encounter a person in need, no matter what he looks like or how he is behaving, we should try gently to ask if he knows where he will spend eternity and try to lead him or her to faith in Jesus Christ as Savior and Lord, not trusting in his or her works but in the finished work of the cross. My experience also forever changed the way I respond to and care for people, whether saved or unsaved.

God established our path and numbered our days before we were ever in our mother's womb (Psalm 139). He has a wonderful purpose for each of us. But we will never fulfill that purpose until we submit our lives to Christ and allow the Father to lead us by His Spirit straight into the glorious plan He has for us. To me, the saddest thing on earth is unfulfilled purpose. God has placed a wealth of treasure within each person to help him or her fulfill his or her God-given future. Because of this, when I look at people, I see prophets, evangelists, teachers, pastors, and apostles. I see the limitless ability of the Spirit to mold and shape them so they can fulfill God's plan and purpose for their lives. I see great potential in each one, because God has a plan for each individual.

On another occasion, while waiting for my car to be detailed, a small boy, about three years old, came into the establishment and sat across from me. As I watched him intently, the compassion of God began to well up in my spirit. When I prayed for his future, my tears began to flow heavier and heavier. I remember saying to the Lord, "No not here!" But God never considers our location when moving our hearts to pray. As I allowed the Spirit of God to move through me, I remember thinking how hard it is for the Lord to allow even one human being to choose death. This tremendously challenged my heart and my commitment to preach the gospel, as I again realized the great responsibility we have to reach out to a hurting and lost world; to tell them of a wonderful Savior who died so that they could live, and the wonderful Father who only wants to bless them and do them good all the days of their lives.

Most people, today, live in a dry, desolate land. They cry out for peace but find none. They look for love and happiness, but their hearts are empty. Their lives seem so futile that they can't even begin to understand that they can make different choices and change their future.

This great spiritual void transcends every fiber of society. Some of the wealthiest people, who seemingly have it all, are so morally and spiritually bankrupt that their lives are, by their own admission, meaningless. On the other side of the spectrum, there are people who have lost everything–spouses, children, homes, possessions, and jobs. Or perhaps they never had anything to begin with, growing up in despair.

All search for answers and help from anyone and anything that might seem hopeful, wandering aimlessly at the gates of hell in a spiritual chaos, blindly waiting for life's next blow. The common thread among them is that somewhere along the way, they lost their hope, their drive, their desire. Perhaps they never had it, or they seemed to have purpose until they obtained everything they thought wealth would bring and discovered that they still felt empty.

As I considered these things, I accepted a mandate from God to reach out to those who are hurting and lost and tell them that there is love, peace, and contentment in Christ. I long to share with them how He fills a void that no amount of money or possessions can ever satisfy and that Jesus came to give them life and to give it abundantly (John 10:10). The kind of life Jesus gives us is described in Matthew 16:25, "Whoever loses his life for My sake will find it." This life Jesus was referring to is "sozo" life; which in the Greek means *to save, to preserve, to make whole*. I want people to know that this is what He desires for us, to be whole.

I began to visit places where the lost and hurting could be found– prisons, transitional homes, and homeless shelters. I told anyone who would listen about this wonderful Savior who redeemed my life out of the pit and changed me.

Since then, I've met just about every type of person imaginable. I've met the rich person who had lost it all, the professional who became crack-addicted and ended up on the streets turning tricks. I've met teachers, bankers, housewives, mothers, daughters, and sisters who lived in despair. Others have been horribly abused and thrown away like garbage. They are hurt and angry, using substances and violence to try to make their existence bearable.

Many beautiful stories have arisen from the ashes of damaged lives, when desperate people looked to Jesus, and He turned their tragedy into triumph.

Chapter 2

SO WHAT IS HOPE?

Everywhere I minister, whether in prisons, homeless shelters, safe houses for women, the church, or around the world, many can quote Jeremiah 29:11, "For I know the thoughts that I think toward you, says the LORD, thoughts of peace and not of evil, to give you a future and a hope." I've often thought this so unusual because the majority of those quoting these words seem to have no fruit of it in their lives. Many times I've asked myself why these people, who seem to know the Word, have no victory in their lives. Do they not know that God's Word is effective? It is sharper than any two-edged sword and able to divide between that which is soul and that which is spirit. Obviously, this promise of God is just rolling around in their heads and has not yet become rooted in their hearts. Amazingly, they have not taken the next step of faith by expecting God to fulfill that which He has spoken.

Why does this Scripture mean so much to the brokenhearted? What does it really mean to them in their hearts? Is it just a wise saying that gets them through from one day to the next, never bringing about lasting change? Is it something they think God will do for everyone else and not for them personally? Or is it really a message of hope that gives them a glimmer of light at the end of a dark tunnel?

Let's take a look at why this Scripture is so powerful and why it is so important to help people see the reality of what God is saying and how this passage can greatly impact their lives.

First, let's talk about the end of the verse—a future and a hope. What is hope? Hope is defined as an earnest expectation of future good. If there is no hope, there is no earnest expectation of future good. When people lose their hope, they emotionally sit down and ultimately become paralyzed. They stop trying, they give up, they quit, and they end up in despair. When people have no hope, they lose their way, because they can't see a future for themselves or their family. Sadly, this condition has affected generations of people. When a child is born into a family of despair, more often than not, his life will end up in the same despair as that of the family.

I have pondered how our level of hope strongly impacts our future success and how our outlook on life strongly influences our success or failure. Expectation cannot be present in one who has no desire for the future. Individuals who lack an expectation for the future exist day by day, never expecting one day to be better than the next. This lack of an expectation of the future is linked with a lack of hope.

Proverbs 13:12 says, "Hope deferred makes the heart sick." The word *sick* means to become weak and wounded, grieved, and afflicted. What this Scripture reveals is that people without hope are weak, wounded, grieved, and afflicted. They are just like the man God brought to my mind at the prayer conference years ago.

When the Bible talks about tragedy and terrible consequences, it also provides instructions on how to help avoid tragic consequences. The second part of Proverbs 13:12 reveals the benefit of hope, "When the desire comes [or you could say, when hope is realized], it is a tree of life." A tree of life is one of continual blessing. When hope is realized, a continual blessing flows from it. Jeremiah 17:7–8 also talks about a healthy, growing tree, "Blessed is the man who trusts in the LORD, and whose hope is the LORD. For he shall be like a tree planted by the waters, which spreads out its roots by the river, and will not fear when heat comes; but its leaf will be green, and will not be anxious in the year of drought, nor will cease from yielding fruit." This analogy that compares a man or woman to a tree, demonstrates the result of hope placed in God. This tree is like a man, woman, or child who, no matter the circumstances, test, or trial, will remain strong, steady, and fruitful to the end. Each time hope is realized, the roots of that tree sink down deeper, establishing faith, patience, and love, which teach us as believers how to respond to adversity.

Hope cannot be placed in what is seen but only in what is not seen. If it can be seen, we already know it exists, so no hope or faith is required. Romans 8:25 tells us that hope produces an eagerness to wait. Hope expects that what is not seen will be seen at a future time and place. Patient hope will never disappoint (Romans 5:5). One of the greatest passages about hope in the Bible is Hebrews 11:1, "Faith is the substance of things hoped for, the evidence of things not seen." We can see through these Scriptures that hope is energized when we believe things can turn out differently than they have in the past or differently from what they are right now. Our future can be bright when we realize that our circumstances can change at any moment and that God's plan for our future is good. In fact, 2 Corinthians 4:17–18 says, "For our light affliction, which is but for a moment, is working for us a far more exceeding and eternal weight of glory, while we do not look at the things which are seen, but at the things which are not seen. For the things which are seen are temporary, but the things which are not seen are eternal."

We must help others to put their hope in God. Hope that is firmly anchored in God will never fail. Hebrews 6:19 confirms this, saying, "This hope we have as an anchor of the soul, both sure and steadfast …." We serve a mighty God who created the universe, and nothing is too hard for Him. We must learn to place our hope fully in Him who is able to do exceedingly, abundantly, above all we could ask or think (Eph. 3:20).

The Apostle Paul knew well the spiritual force of hope. In Philippians 1:19–20, while imprisoned in Rome, he said, "For I know that this will turn out for my deliverance through your prayer and the supply of the Spirit of Jesus Christ, according to my earnest expectation and hope that in nothing I shall be ashamed." He boldly declared that he knew he would be delivered, not only because of the prayers of the saints but also, more importantly, according to his own earnest expectation and hope of a good future.

Hope must be squarely placed on the Lord. The benefits of hope are tremendous. As we have just seen, hope ensures our deliverance. Hope also brings rest (Psalm 16:9). And hope strengthens us to endure (Psalm 31:24).

I have often wondered why so many live defeated lives when God has such a wonderful plan for each of us. What are they lacking that prevents an earnest expectation of good for their future? Why are so many living without hope?

Chapter 3

THE NEED FOR VISION

My belief is that, regardless of where people come from or the circumstances in which they find themselves, the missing ingredient is vision. Vision is the ability to believe that one has a future to look forward to.

Proverbs 29:18 says, "Where there is no vision the people perish" (KJV). When we believe that a good future awaits us, our hope is renewed, and our dreams and desires come alive again.

Vision sparks passion in the heart.
Passion is a driving force that will propel each one of us
into the place God has called us to be.

Vision plays a powerful, vital, and pivotal part in hope. Without hope there can be no future, and without the ability to anticipate a future, there will be no hope. The ability to anticipate the future is perhaps one of the most vital and powerful forces in an individual's life.

Besides being the ability to believe that one has a future to look forward to, vision can involve a mental picture of something desired. Perhaps a person going to college to prepare to become a teacher envisions herself as a teacher in a future classroom full of students.

Vision requires an understanding of the gifts, talents, and abilities possessed that will produce the desire. Vision further requires an understanding that God is in control, and by His grace, and His grace alone, we will fulfill the purpose He desires for our lives. When understanding is coupled with the strength and stability of Christ, there is no limit to where our hope will take us.

Faith also works with vision. If you believe it, you will begin to see it, you will expect it and watch for it, and it will surely come to pass. Each of us is drawn toward what we believe, moving continually closer to our heart's desire.

Vision turns on a light in the eyes of those who have lost hope. Once they begin to see that there is a future containing something meaningful that they can do, the light comes on, and a "yes" resounds in their soul. Light is also the expression in someone's eye that says, "I believe!"

Sometimes vision brings a deep revelation or understanding of the gifts and abilities that reside inside each person. I will never forget the light that came on in the eyes of twenty-five women during a session I taught at a local jail. Many thought they would never be able to do anything worthwhile. They were drug addicts, prostitutes, and the like, thinking this is all they would ever be, believing, *This is it, there is nothing else.* No hope, just pure desperation and emptiness.

During the meeting, I had each complete a four-question career aptitude test to determine what careers would best suit them. This simple test also included information regarding the personality of the one who would best be suited for a particular career. As we went through the results one by one, it was amazing to see their expressions change as their eyes lit up. Many laughed at the thought of being lawyers, computer programmers, or journalists. They had never thought that kind of potential resided just below the surface within them.

The best part is that their lives are not over. There's still time to get it together, go to school, and obtain the dreams and desires of their lives. It's never too late. In fact, the calling and gift of God is irrevocable—He will never take it back.

The enemy has nothing new to throw at us, all he can do is twist the Word, the will, and the plan of God. He can only pervert the plans of God! The most amazing thing, though, is that he will never be successful in completely thwarting the plan of God. He can only hinder by obstruction. The devil's ultimate plan is to take the very gift of God in each of us and pervert it for his own use in the kingdom of darkness. Many of the women, in the prison system, who are so messed up were themselves gifted by God to be a part of upholding the very law they had chosen to break.

Oh, but God! He has already told us that the gifts of God are lasting. The gifts in each person will always lie in wait for our thoughts to become agreeable with His will. How exciting it is to see people realize their potential and walk in the plan of God for their lives. How do they get there? They get there by developing their ability to anticipate their future according to God's plan.

One of the most powerful sayings about vision comes to us from a minor prophet in the Old Testament. God Himself spoke to Habakkuk regarding the judgment that was coming to the Israelites by the hands of the Babylonians, whom God used as a tool in His hand. Habakkuk cried out to God in chapter one asking for help, and God answered him, making sure that Habakkuk knew that what God promised would be fulfilled. In Habakkuk 2:2–4, God said, "Write the vision and make it plain on tablets, that he may run who reads it. For the vision is yet for an appointed time; but at the end it will speak, and it will not lie. Though it tarries, wait for it; because it will surely come, it will not tarry. Behold the proud, his soul is not upright in him; but the just shall live by his faith." In this scripture we learn something powerful about how to achieve our future. When we have a dream in our heart we should write it down, just like God instructed Habakkuk. This is a very powerful thing to do. I have known and heard of individuals who wrote their dreams down, only later on to experience the fulfillment of the very thing they dreamed of. One such famous individual is the comedian/actor Jim Carrey. He dreamed of making it big in the entertainment industry. Once he did, he shared that he had been carrying a check around in his wallet for many years. This check was payable to him in the amount of twenty million dollars. He believed one day he would receive a check for that amount, and now he has received many times more than this amount. Another instance was a young professional man who had a near death experience. He decided that life was too short and precarious. Since he wasn't sure how many days he would have in this life, he decided to make a list of the things he dreamed about doing and then go about doing them. When he made the list he had no idea that he would be able to experience each, but within six years every dream was marked off his list. Now he keeps a list of everything he desires to do. God's Word may have been given to individuals in the Bible for their specific situation, but it can also be applied to our everyday life. Paul said in 2 Timothy 3:16–17, "All Scripture is given by inspiration of God, and is profitable for doctrine, for reproof, for correction, for instruction in righteousness, that the man of God may be complete, thoroughly equipped for every good work." And God delights to give us the desires of our heart, as long as we remain open and pliable in our hearts toward Him (Psalm 37:4, paraphrased). In Habakkuk's, God gives us powerful instruction for life and then tells us to wait for the things we hope for, even watch for them. One thing we see in verse four is that it takes faith to see the fulfillment of our future. We must trust God and know that He is in control of our future and He will surely bring His plan for us to pass.

Remember, hope was defined as an earnest expectation of future good. Vision must be accompanied by a belief that the future will be good. We must learn that God is good, and He wants to do us good. He has a good plan and a good path to get us to where we are going. Psalm 119:68 declares of God, "You are good and do good." The simple fact that God is not going to intervene in our lives by overtaking our wills and forcing us into His plan indicates that He is waiting for each of us to put our trust and hope in Him. We must believe that God is good in order to expect good in our life.

Let's think for a moment, God loved each of us so much that He sent His only Son to die so that we could live forever in heaven. And Jesus, His Son, did not resist the Father's desire to send Him. He was ready and willing to come. He longed to come and set us free. He wants to do us good, and He is waiting for us to open the door and invite Him in. Once He's in our lives, we must trust and believe that His desired good for us will come to pass. This is the hope of our future!

We find two powerful examples of vision demonstrated in the lives of people from the Bible. How hard is it to believe the things that look impossible? Think of Joseph in the book of Genesis. He had a dream, a dream God gave him. He believed the dream and became so excited about it that he shared the dream with some family members. They became jealous of Joseph and plotted to kill him, even saying, "Let's kill him and then see what comes of his dream!" While Joseph had a vision of his future and those around him tried to destroy him, he never let go of his vision or his desire for the future. He held onto it in prison and as a slave, and it eventually came to pass for all to see.

Another example is Mary, the mother of Jesus, who was visited by an angel who announced that she would give birth to the Son of God. We too must believe like Joseph and Mary that with God nothing shall be impossible (Matt. 17:20). When people gain the ability to anticipate a positive future, hopeless hearts change direction. Eyes are lifted up, and expectations begin to change. But how will hopeless people know there is a future? How can they begin to expect change to come into their lives? Just like the women I minister to in the prison, they must be told. Someone must come alongside them and tell them there is a different way. Someone must say, "I believe in you and know that there is a better way." God will send a messenger to them. Could that messenger be you?

Chapter 4 ❧

CREATED TO COMMUNICATE

What is our part then? To reach out to those lost in despair. To tell them there is a future and a hope. To help them give birth to the vision God has for their life. How can we do this? By sharing the love of God and the message of hope with every person who comes across our path! We are agents of action for God's plan and purpose. We are God's messengers! One of my favorite Scriptures breaks this down so beautifully.

> Whoever believes on Him will not be put to shame. For there is no distinction between Jew and Greek, for the same Lord over all is rich to all who call upon Him. For whoever calls on the name of the LORD shall be saved.
>
> How then shall they call on Him in whom they have not believed? And how shall they believe in Him of whom they have not heard? And how shall they hear without a preacher? And how shall they preach unless they are sent? As it is written: "How beautiful are the feet of those who preach the gospel of peace, who bring glad tidings of good things!"
>
> (Rom. 10:11–15)

I can't help but think how beautiful were the feet of Mary Magdalene as she ran from the empty tomb of Jesus to declare the good news to

His disciples, "He is risen" (Matt. 28:7). How beautiful were the feet of the woman at the well when she went to her countrymen and declared, "Come and see" (John 4:29).

The word *beautiful* in Romans 10:15 does not describe the physical appearance of the feet. In the Greek, this word is figurative and means being on time and in season. What does it mean to be "in season"? This phrase means that the words come at the right moment in our life. Proverbs 25:11 declares, "A word fitly spoken is like apples of gold, in settings of silver." A timely word that is exactly what a person needs to hear is worth far more than earthly treasures.

How do we encourage those who need help? Very simply—keep hope alive by reminding each person that God has a good plan for his or her future. Help him or her see that the future can be better than the past. Point out peoples' talents and abilities, then give them opportunities to use them. Walk alongside each one until he or she can walk on his or her own. Encourage the person continually by affirming your love and awareness of his or her gifts. Encouragement helps to adjust self worth and ultimately to enable vision.

My message is a simple one: You are a messenger, and you have been sent to deliver a word of life to those living in desolate places. They are all around you, and perhaps you are caught in this trap of despair. To help yourself and others around you, always be full of God's goodness and ready to deliver a word at the appropriate time to those lost in despair.

God-inspired and love-motivated communication is paramount when reaching out to the brokenhearted. The gospel of Jesus Christ and the love of God will not be known if no one communicates and demonstrates it. Paul mentioned its importance in Romans 10:14. The New Living Translation says it best, "How can they believe in Him if they have never heard about Him? And how can they hear about Him unless someone tells them?" Matthew 24:14 declares the gospel will be preached or communicated in the entire world, and then the end will come. We are to be witnesses who tell others about Jesus based on our own experience with Him and the Bible's teachings.

What is a witness? Are we, the family of God, born-again believers, not witnesses who testify or communicate about Jesus to those around us? Communication does not occur through words alone. Our lives communicate God's goodness and faithfulness to those who believe. Listening is an important form of communication, and body language is another.

But the most powerful form of communication is the spoken word. It's no surprise that communication is what the enemy attacks most. If he can pervert what is being said, or even what is being heard, the perception of it, he can prevent people from receiving the message of salvation. Many people speak of how hard it is to talk with someone they don't know or to speak in front of a crowd. These are two different situations, but both are important ways to communicate the message of Christ. Sometimes, because we have a fear of speaking to people we don't know, we just don't speak at all. The enemy has sold the body of Christ a false bill of goods to force our mouths shut, because he knows the key to deliverance resides in the mouth. People desperately need to hear the good news of Jesus Christ. The enemy has placed an invisible barrier between the lost and the saved. We have to step out of our comfort zone to deliver the message and communicate the gospel. Our fears and feelings of inadequacy keep us from people who would be eternally grateful to hear a good word. Therefore, it is imperative, even urgent, that we begin to share with everyone who comes across our path.

Words help create an atmosphere for God to move in. The power of life and death are in the tongue. God used words to create. God's Word framed the world (Hebrews 11:3). When He said, "Let there be light" (Gen. 1:3), light was created and continues to be. In the Hebrew language, the word *man* in Genesis means "speaking spirit." We were created in God's image, so our words, like His, also create. They create and shape our lives. Even the secular arena confirms this principle in what Robert K. Merton, a well-known sociologist of the twentieth century, called a "self-fulfilling prophecy." He proposed that whatever is spoken over and over again in one's life will eventually become true. For example, if a child is told over and over again that he is stupid, eventually he will believe it and the spoken words will come to pass. Whatever you believe you are is what you will ultimately become. "For as he [man] thinks in his heart, so is he" (Prov. 23:7). Many people struggling with some of life's most devastating circumstances have believed a lie about themselves. This is why it is so crucial to tell people about their potential in Christ.

It is time NOW for those of us who know Him to begin communicating with everyone around us about who He is and what He has done for mankind. Carpe diem! Seize the day! We must seize every moment and take every opportunity to communicate the good news of Jesus Christ.

Imagine for a moment that you don't believe there could be anything good in your future until someone comes along and tells you that your future is bright and good things are about to happen. At first, you might respond, "Yeah right, that will never happen!" But, as you continue to hear about the good future planned for you, you begin to believe that maybe, just maybe there might be a possibility of something good happening to you. It takes time to retrain our thought lives. This is why it is so important that we continually tell those around us how gifted they are and how wonderful their future will be. We can't just tell people those things and expect that their lives will change overnight. We have to stay with them and walk through situations with them, telling them and showing them that their lives can be different.

Psalm 78 tells us that God has established His testimony so that future generations will have hope. It's God's testimony, His Word that gives hope to future generations. As witnesses of God's promises, we are the ones who will lead others into the same testimony that someone else led us in. Our lives speak, and of course, our words have impact. It's time to step into the plan of God for our lives and begin communicating to everyone around us. Let's do it!

Chapter 5

WHY HESITATE?

We've seen that hope is the key to igniting vision in a person's life. We've talked about the importance of communication to help people realize their future. Now let's look at the reasons why we hesitate to share the good news and step into the ministry God has called us to.

Fear—Our Invisible Foe

Fear is one of the greatest issues people struggle with when trying to share the gospel or minister to those in need. We also struggle with rejection when someone rejects Christ. What if someone asks a question we don't know the answer to? And what if the person wants more from us than we are willing to give?

Fear is the opposite of faith, and when we are fearful we are more focused on our own abilities than on God's ability. When we are in faith, we are more focused on God's ability than our own. So the easiest way to get rid of fear is to put our focus on God's ability.

Let also look at what the Scriptures have to say about fear.

1 John 4:18 says, "There is no fear in love; but perfect love casts out fear, because fear involves torment. But he who fears has not been made perfect in love."

If perfect love casts out fear and I am struggling with fear right now, my love needs to be perfected or made perfect so that I can overcome fear. How can I determine where my love needs to be perfected?

First, take a look at your love toward others. 1 John 4:12 says, "If we love one another, God abides in us, and His love has been perfected in us." And Proverbs 17:17 declares, "A friend loves at all times." Jesus gave each of us a new commandment in John 13:34–35. He said, "A new commandment I give to you, that you love one another; as I have loved you, that you also love one another."

Ask yourself some questions. Am I walking in love toward those around me? How am I responding to those who mistreat me? Be honest and open with yourself. If you are failing the love test in any way, ask the Holy Spirit to bring change to your life. Yield yourself to Him, and allow Him to perfect your heart towards others.

Second, test your life by God's definition of love in 1 Corinthians 13—love is not envious, jealous, boastful, vainglorious, conceited, arrogant, prideful, rude, unmannerly, insistent of its own way or right, self-seeking, touchy, fretful, or resentful. Love does not rejoice at injustice, act unbecomingly, or display itself haughtily. Love, the God kind of love, endures, is patient, kind, takes no account of evil done, pays no attention to a suffered wrong, rejoices when right and truth prevail, bears up under anything, is ever ready to believe the best of every person, hopes in all circumstances, endures everything without weakening, and never fails, fades out or becomes obsolete.

If any of these areas are love issues in your life, repent and ask God to help you love every individual with the love He has for that person.

If your love toward others is not an issue, you need to know that fear is an invisible foe to believers. It's like an imaginary barrier that when crossed, disappears never to be seen or felt again. It takes faith to step over our fear, and it only takes one step to conquer it. Never allow fear to stop you from obeying God and reaching out to love people. Even if you are in a very scary situation, God will protect you. Destroy fear in your life by doing exactly what you are afraid to do.

Lack of Bible Knowledge

The best way to present the gospel is by sharing your own personal testimony of how you received salvation, how God brought you out of your former situation and showed you His goodness. For me, it was the peace of God that I saw on the faces of people who knew Him that drew me into a relationship with Christ. When I share my faith, I often talk about how my life was devoid of inner peace, and when I recognized true peace I became desperate to receive it. Once I did, I wanted more and more.

Many verses throughout the Bible talk of how we receive our salvation. It's these Scriptures that we can study and memorize so that we can lead others into a relationship with Jesus. Let's look at a few.

First, we must admit that we are sinners. Romans 3:23 reveals, "All have sinned and fall short of the glory of God." Then we must repent and ask for forgiveness. Acts 3:19 is a good reference for the results of repentance, "Repent therefore and be converted, that your sins may be blotted out, so that times of refreshing may come from the presence of the Lord." God is waiting for us to come to Him so He can restore life back to us.

All it takes to receive salvation is outlined in Romans 10:9–10, "If you confess with your mouth the Lord Jesus and believe in your heart that God has raised Him from the dead, you will be saved. For with the heart one believes unto righteousness, and with the mouth confession is made unto salvation." People go astray by thinking that their way to "enlightenment" is better than the way God has prepared. But Proverbs 16:25 clearly shows us, "There is a way that seems right to a man, but its end is the way of death."

We were always in need of a Savior, and only Jesus, the one who was without sin, could ultimately pay the price for a sinner. When His work on the cross was finished, there was no longer a need for sacrifice. To receive eternal life, one only needs to receive Jesus as the Lord and Savior of his or her life. And never forget, there is only one way to be reconciled to the Father, and that's through a relationship with the Son, Jesus Christ.

These Scriptures, along with your personal testimony, will help you present the gospel. Describe events where God's unconditional love for you revealed His faithfulness and goodness toward those He calls His own. People are searching for what is real, and being able to hear from someone who has an experience with the Lord is invaluable to those who need to make a decision about where they will spend eternity.

Overcoming fear and learning Bible verses to help you share your testimony of what God has done in your life will help you become bold in sharing the most wonderful news ever—God loves people and has good plans for them!

Let Your Light Shine

Besides telling others about what God has done for us and wants to do for them, we also need to live the way God wants us to live if we are to draw others to Him. Jesus declared in Matthew 5:16, "Let your light so shine before men, that they may see your good works and glorify your Father in heaven."

The whole world is watching the church and followers of Christ to see if what we believe is really true. They are watching to see if we are going to live our lives in a way that demonstrates Christ's teaching. Because of our powerful ability to witness to the world by the way we live, we must watch what we do, being careful to follow Christ's teaching, and allowing our lives to testify of the truth of God's promises.

This is of utmost importance, because if we preach one message and then live in a completely different way, we make God's Word of no effect. We also make ourselves hypocrites in the eyes of the world.

The world is our stage, and if we show evidence through our lives of the goodness of God, we will be tools for God to use to draw all men to Himself. In the book of Romans, Paul taught the believers that they should not despise the riches of God's goodness, forbearance, and longsuffering, because it was these very things, when manifested in the lives of God's people, that would lead people to repentance (Romans 2:4, paraphrased). When we are ashamed of the gospel and hide our commitment to Him when we are with certain people, we actually help turn them away from, instead of toward God.

As we realize and acknowledge the things that make us hesitate to share or communicate the gospel with those around us, we can ask God to help us and yield our hearts to the Holy Spirit so that He can do the work in us necessary to prepare us for ministry.

Simply pray for liberty to communicate, and study God's Word to fill your heart with truth. Then the next time someone comes across your path who needs a life-giving word or testimony, you will be ready and able to share. In addition to communication and helping people on our own, we can get involved in outreach ministry at our church. We can also look for opportunities to minister to the hurting and broken in our community, and find a way to reach out to them.

No matter where God stations us for the lost, we need to know some vital keys for effectiveness in ministry. The next chapter deals with these keys, and when you apply them in your life, you will see fruit not only your life but also in the lives of those to whom you minister.

SEVEN KEYS FOR EFFECTIVE OUTREACH MINISTRY

Often in ministry we see people who have given their all for the lost lose their zeal for the gospel. I've often seen this and have asked the Lord why it is that people who are so passionate for the unsaved can one day see these same people as burdens, eventually walking away from the ministry.

Sometimes we allow the needs of the lost to dominate our efforts to help, trying to meet every need and thus becoming overburdened and ineffective in ministry. The Lord has reminded me that not until we get to heaven will every human need be met. If God's plan were to fulfill every human need, there would be no need on earth. When healing was needed, it would always occur. When we need additional finances, they would always come. What moves the hand of God is His Word and our belief in His Word. If we allow the needs of the people to overwhelm us, we will eventually lose our vigor and drive to minister the gospel, because our eyes are on the wrong thing.

Let's look at some foundational keys that will help us stay strong in ministry and be effective as we endeavor to be God's heart, hands, feet, and mouth to a hurting world. As we learn these and grow strong in the application of them, we will truly rise up and be the army God has called us to be.

Love Unconditionally

We are charged by God Himself to always believe the best of every person! How many times have we read 1 Corinthians 13 and spoken of love as defined by this Scripture? This part of Scripture is actually a definition of God's love toward us. Extending love is sometimes inconvenient when it costs us time, effort, or emotional energy. But inconvenient as it can be, love is God's language. Wherever we find ourselves reaching out to others, we are not there because people are lost. Yes, people are lost and we are to go and gather them. But our reason for reaching them is His great love for them, of which we are messengers. In the times in which we live, it will be the demonstration of love that speaks the loudest to those who need help. We should always love in word, but more importantly we must also love in deed. 1 John 3:16–20 exhorts believers in this:

> By this we know love, because He laid down His life for us. And we also ought to lay down our lives for the brethren. But whoever has this world's goods, and sees his brother in need, and shuts up his heart from him, how does the love of God abide in him? My little children, let us not love in word or in tongue, but in deed and in truth. And by this we know that we are of the truth, and shall assure our hearts before Him.

Our lives should demonstrate the power of God's love in this way. The power demonstrated in God's love transforms your ability to minister, when you learn to walk in that power. I remember the first time I read this part of Scripture in the Amplified Bible. It was like an explosion in my spirit. I thought, *This is it–this is the blueprint for power in our lives when we walk in the love of God!*

Philippians 1:9–10 (AMP) perfectly defines the power of God's love in Paul's prayer for the church at Philippi:

> And this I pray: that your love may abound yet more and more and extend to its fullest development in knowledge and all keen insight [that your love may display itself in greater depth of acquaintance and more comprehensive discernment], *so that you may surely learn to* sense what is vital, and approve and prize what is excellent and of real value

[recognizing the highest and the best, and distinguishing the moral differences], and that you may be untainted and pure and unerring and blameless [so that with hearts unsullied, you may approach] the day of Christ [not stumbling nor causing others to stumble].

When God's love is perfected in us, we will walk in power. We will learn to sense what is vital, approve and prize what is excellent and of real value, recognize the highest and best, and distinguish between what is right and what is wrong. As we learn to walk in this love power, it will produce the following fruit in our life: increased knowledge, keen insight, greater depth of acquaintance with others, deeper and more insightful discernment. And we will truly become the image of Christ to the world.

Ephesians 2:10 says that we are His workmanship. In 2 Corinthians 3:2–3, Paul declares that we are living epistles and that through our daily living we will become like a letter written by Christ to the world. What was the message Christ came to confirm? God's amazing love. We ourselves are becoming His own declaration of love to the world. I like to think of this letter as a love poem written on our hearts to all of mankind. The Message paraphrase puts it best, "Your very lives are a letter that anyone can read by just looking at you. Christ himself wrote it—not with ink, but with God's living Spirit; not chiseled into stone, but carved into human lives—and we publish it."

The beauty of this amazing love should also be seen in us. 2 Corinthians 2:14–15 says, "Through us diffuses the fragrance of His knowledge in every place. For we are to God the fragrance of Christ among those who are being saved and among those who are perishing." The word *diffuse* in the Greek literally means *to appear*. It also means to manifest, to show, and to declare. As we love those around us, we will demonstrate God's love for them.

To love others, we must guard against judging others. Everything we think and say should be motivated by the love of God. This will prevent judgment from rising up in our hearts. Romans 12:15–19 outlines parameters for dealing with others, giving us a code of ethics, or discipline, for life.

By sharing in the joy of others, we show our love (Romans 12:15 and Isaiah 66:10). We also show our love when we weep with those who weep. Our love for others will cause us to feel what they are feeling. This is an outward sign of our deep compassion and desire to help.

Many times Paul exhorted believers to be in unity, with singleness of mind and spirit (Romans 12:16). What is the singleness of our mind to be toward? Christ! If our purpose is the same and we share in everything together, then our witness will be powerful. Our love and compassion for one another will speak volumes to those we desire to minister to. At all costs, guard unity among you!

Keep your eyes focused on Jesus (v. 16). When Jesus is the center of what you are doing, you will do things for the right reason. When He is your purpose for reaching out to people, you will demonstrate His love and desire greatly for each person to come to know Him.

Be friends with the humble (v. 16). When you remain humble, you will never think you are the wise one. No one has all the answers, and no one really needs our opinion. People need the gospel. They need God's Word, and they need to know He is real. They need to experience the supernatural power of God and know Jesus as friend. If we are proud and opinionated and walking around like we think we've got all the answers, we put people off rather than help to create a desire in them to know our God. When we are humble and demonstrate God's love and goodness, they will want our God. In fact, they will be jealous for our God because of the great joy and peace in which His people walk.

Always be like Jesus to people. Act like He acts and do what He does. When we set our hearts to do this, we will never entertain thoughts of evil (v. 17). When someone does or says something offensive, don't judge or respond in kind. Just go on loving and believing the best of the person. God will work it out, and when He does, the outcome will be beautiful.

Remember that people are watching what you do and listening to what you say. At first, they watch because they want to prove wrong the things you are saying. If you are consistent in living your life the way God desires, before long those people are going to be coming to you for help. They will trust you because you have proven that you belong to God, because your life is a demonstration of His goodness.

As much as it is within your power, live peaceably with all men (v. 18). It is said that peace is the manifest presence of God. Strife is the manifest presence of the devil. As Christians, we should be peacemakers, instruments of God to bring peace in every situation. We should be able to point people in the direction of peace no matter what is going on in their lives. James said this so beautifully in James 3:18, "Now the fruit of righteousness is sown in peace by those who make peace."

He is literally saying that the fruit of our life in God should be sown in peace. We should be establishing peace and bringing peace to every situation we encounter. In 1993, when I was finding my way back to God, it was the peace I saw on the faces of those who knew Him that drew me back. I remember saying to the Lord, "I want that!" Thank God I found it, and today there is nothing that I would allow to steal my peace.

Paul said very simply that each of us should behave like a Christian. Act like you know the Lord. Remember those you hang around with are those you will act like. When you hang around Jesus, you will act like Him. Endeavor to know Him, and then treat people just like He would. Then they will desire to know our God, and an open door for the gospel to be preached will stand wide.

Pray with Power and Perseverance

Prayer has the power to change everything. It opens the door for God to move in our lives and in the lives of those we pray for, because we are demonstrating agreement with His will. Never forsake this tool; pray before if you have time, pray during, pray after trying to help those in need. Prayer prepares us for ministry; prayer guides us during ministry; and prayer seals the plans of God. Never leave a person without praying for him or her. It is the single most powerful thing God's servants have to offer, other than the name of Jesus.

Let's look at some the tools of prayer that play a powerful part in establishing God's plan in the lives of people.

The Power of the Spoken Word

Every word from God that is prayed will come to pass. In 2001, I traveled to India as part of a mission team. While preparing for the trip, the Lord impressed upon my heart a scripture from the book of Job in chapter 22. Verse 28 says, "You will also declare a thing, and it will be established for you."

The Lord also impressed on my heart to declare His Word over every person I came in contact with during the India mission. Isaiah 55:11 reveals a powerful truth: God's Word will not return to Him void. It will prosper in the thing for which He sent it. This gives us a key to the power released when we pray God's Word. What I mean by this is to take the Scripture and make it personal either to yourself or those you are praying for. One of my favorite scriptures to pray comes out of the book of Ephesians in 1:18. The scripture says, "The eyes of your understanding being enlightened; that you may know what is the hope of His calling, what are the riches of the glory of His inheritance in the saints." When I pray this for a person who needs to know the Lord or understand something, I will insert the person's name I am praying for in place of the word *you* or *your*. For example, using my name, "I pray that Charlana's eyes would be enlightened that she would know the hope of His calling." When I learned to pray using the Scripture in this way, I saw great change come into my life and the lives of those I prayed for. I will never forget the faces of those I prayed for, and for many of them, I will never forget what was declared over their lives. The words were not mine, but His, because they came from His Word. And they will come to pass.

Be still, and listen to what God is saying in your heart. Then as you pray, proclaim what God has impressed upon your heart for that person's life. God will watch over it, and He will perform it in his or her life. When we get to heaven, we will hear the wonderful, glorious things God did as a result of a simple prayer using the power of God's Word.

The effective, fervent, heartfelt prayer of a righteous man avails much (James 5:16, AMP). *Avail* means *to have force, be of strength, be whole*. It means to give the advantage or to help. When we pray, we ask God, even open the door to Him, to get involved in whatever is going on in our life. Wherever God is involved in our life we have the advantage for success. It invites God to move, and He will only move when He is invited to.

The Power of Agreement

Do not miss any opportunity to agree in prayer with someone for what he or she believes God to do in his or her life or family. We read in Matthew 18:19–20, "Again I say to you that if two of you agree on earth concerning anything that they ask, it will be done for them by My Father in heaven. For where two or three are gathered together in My name, I am there in the midst of them." Everyone has a situation that needs to change in his life. Asking what you can agree in prayer for will open the door to ministry.

It has been my experience that most people want prayer. All we have to do is ask the individual if there is something we can agree in prayer for, he or she will respond with a situation, or even a list of things, he or she needs God to do in his or her life. This is our open door to pray in agreement with God's Word. The scriptures I always pray for regarding personal situations, outside of the request for immediate needs, are related to wisdom. In Colossians 1:9 we see Paul praying about wisdom for the church at Colosse. He says to the leader of the church that he doesn't cease to pray for him that he may be filled with the knowledge of God's will in all wisdom and spiritual understanding. No matter what is going on in our lives, we need the wisdom of God to know His will. Then further we need to know what to do and how to do it. God's wisdom will bring the information we need for every situation. Don't just pray in agreement for their needs to be met, but for each one to have the wisdom necessary to make right choices regarding their future.

The Importance of Staying Filled with God's Word

We have nothing to offer except what is of God. Our opinions are as nothing, but God's Word is forever settled—the same yesterday, today, and forever. John 15:7–8 says, "If you abide in Me, and My words abide in you, you will ask what you desire, and it shall be done for you. By this My Father is glorified, that you bear much fruit; so you will be My disciples."

Whenever you are preparing for ministry or getting ready to reach out to someone, spend extra time in the Word, asking the Holy Spirit to guide you. I always find that whatever Scripture is in my heart will be an answer for someone in need. Give time to study the Word and memorize certain scriptures that will be of help to people who need comfort. As you do this, you will be surprised with what comes out of your mouth as you pray for someone. I love the scripture in Psalm 45:1 that illustrates perfectly the person who is filled with good things from the Lord. It reads, "My heart is overflowing with a good theme; I recite my composition concerning the King; My tongue is the pen of a ready writer." What a beautiful picture this paints of an individual whose life if full of God and all that is good of Him. This person is every ready to speak a word in season to him who is weary. This is the life God desires for each of us to live.

The Weapons of our Warfare

We read in 2 Corinthians 10:4 that grace, mercy, faith, truth, peace, righteousness, salvation, and God's Word are the weapons of God's warfare. Outreach ministry must be bathed in prayer and motivated by love. Love gives you the ability and courage to speak. Each one of these weapons of God is an attribute we should demonstrate in our daily living. We should extend grace, have mercy, be full of faith, walk in and minister truth, be peaceable with all men, and live in the righteousness Christ provided for us. As we do, no argument will be able to withstand our efforts to reach the lost.

The Power of the Name of Jesus

Often we pray and at the end say "amen." This is the most ineffective prayer that could be prayed. It may be exactly in line with the will of God and precisely what the individual needs, but because it wasn't asked in the name of Jesus, it falls to the ground dead. Some end their prayers with another sentence that omits the name of Jesus, such as, In Your precious Son's name or In the name of my Lord. We are to pray in the name of Jesus. There is power in the name of Jesus! Pray always in the name of Jesus. Declare the name of Jesus, and invoke His name in every situation. Philippians 2:9–10 says that God has highly exalted Jesus and given Him the name which is above every name, that at the name of Jesus every knee should bow.

It is very clear in the Word that Jesus said to ask in His name. Jesus said in John 14:13, 14–26; 15:16; 16:23–26 to ask in His name. Further, as servants of God, we have received power in the name of Jesus over all the works of the enemy (Luke 10:19). Power there means *authority, jurisdiction, liberty, might, and strength*. When we pray to prepare ourselves or when we pray for others, we must use the authority given to us to stand in that place—in the name of Jesus!

The Power of the Blood

When praying for someone, plead the blood of Jesus over him and his circumstances. Nothing can withstand the force of the blood sacrifice Jesus made for us all. It carries the atonement for every sin, sickness, or bondage that will ever plague mankind. Jesus died once and for all. His work is finished; prayer enforces the victory of Jesus.

Revelation 12:11 says, "And they overcame him by the blood of the Lamb and by the word of their testimony, and they did not love their lives to the death." The blood ensured our victory in every area of life. It is the blood of Jesus that redeems, cleanses, purifies, sanctifies, and makes us whole. It restored us back into intimate fellowship with the Father. Jesus' sacrifice made the way clear for us to return to the Father's presence. Because of the finished work of the cross, we can go boldly into the throne of grace that we may obtain grace in our times of need (Hebrews 4:16).

Be One with the Spirit

Listen with the ears of the Spirit so you can hear what God is saying. Maintain a "Jesus can" attitude. God has something to say. A word spoken fitly and in season can change a person's future. A Scripture that will help build your faith regarding hearing and speaking is Isaiah 50:4, "The Lord GOD has given me the tongue of the learned, that I should know how to speak a word in season to him who is weary. He awakens me morning by morning, He awakens my ear to hear as the learned."

Proverbs gives wonderful knowledge of how these spoken words affect those who hear them. Proverbs 15:23 says a word spoken in due season is good, and when spoken it brings joy to the one who hears it.

Proverbs 24:26 says that a right answer is like a kiss! People need to hear from God. One word from heaven can change a life forever. Where is the one word going to come from? Your mouth!! Hallelujah! God will fill your mouth with His Word, and when you speak it, His Word will have a supernatural effect on the person who hears it.

Paul exhorted us in Ephesians 5:18 to "be filled with the Spirit." How can we stay filled with the Spirit? By spending time in prayer, reading the Scriptures, and meditating on what the Word instructs us to do. As you stayed filled and walk as one with the Spirit, God's words will begin to come easily as you listen to Him. Endeavor to listen so you can hear Him, then speak what He tells you to speak, and you will bless many!

Maintain Boundaries

Knowing and maintaining boundaries in ministry is vital to its effectiveness. Outreach ministry involves people who most often are in need. Sometimes their needs can overwhelm us. When they do, we will find ourselves driven by their needs and not by the vision and purpose of what we are doing. When we become driven by the needs of people, we will violate boundaries in every direction. And we will allow those to whom we minister to violate our boundaries as well. Many years ago I met a woman who was trying to help other ladies being released from prison. She was so driven by their needs that they would whip her into a frenzy trying to get help. Every time I was around this well-meaning woman, she was always in a crisis. When we become driven by the needs of people, we will be consumed by the burden of taking care of them. This is not God's plan for us.

Never stray from the purpose of what you are doing, and stay the course until you are finished. Know your role in the purpose, and do only what you are asked to do. Also, if there are certain parameters given, stay within those parameters. If you lose your purpose, you lose your focus. Eventually what you are doing will become confused. Where confusion is, there is every evil thing.

By staying true to our purpose, we maintain a boundary with those we are trying to help. Not long ago, my husband was asked by someone at our church to take two men back to the Salvation Army after service.

He agreed. Upon arriving at the facility, he said goodbye to the men. One got right out saying, "thank you," and the other one stayed in the truck asking for money. My husband kept telling the man that he wasn't going to give him any money, but the homeless man refused to get out of the vehicle until he got money. Thankfully, the other man came back and convinced him to get out of the truck. My husband's purpose was only to give the men a ride to the Salvation Army and nothing else. Remember, there are people who do things for dishonest reasons.

Sometimes people will ask for money for a specific need. If so, we should never just blindly give people money. If they need gas, you could follow them to a gas station and put gas in the car. If they need food, then give them food, or direct them to a food distribution center in your community. I have personally paid for one night at a hotel for an individual who said she was displaced from home. We can't just receive people at face value. We must use the wisdom and discernment God has given us to verify any information given to make sure the story is true.

Some people will manipulate others to obtain the things they want. They know the system and therefore will work the system for personal gain. When we try to help them, they may try to take advantage of our compassion. We must realize that each person is accountable for their own decisions and actions. The best thing we can do for them is to help them make better choices and teach them how to live this life to the best of their ability with the help of Christ. This will help them become self sufficient in Christ's sufficiency. If you meet every need, you will become his or her source instead of Jesus. As you maintain boundaries and give people a hand up instead of a handout, you will not allow yourself to be put in the position of becoming their deliverer. Jesus is their deliverer, He is also the One who will meet their needs, and we must learn to point people to Him. I've often thought of myself as someone who stands along a highway and gives directions. Just keep pointing him or her in the right direction and helping teach him or her to choose the right direction. As we do this, we empower them with the ability to make right choices on their own, to grow and succeed in life.

Guard against allowing people to become too familiar with you or you becoming too familiar with people. Familiarity breeds contempt. Once a person becomes familiar with you, most often he will not be able to receive further guidance or instruction. A familiar person can no longer receive from the one trying to help or speak into his or her life.

Keep balance and maintain your integrity at all times. The people of God should be the most stable people on the face of the earth. We should also be the most reliable. How can the lost receive help from us if we are as big a mess as they are? Or if we are acting like the rest of the world!

2 Corinthians 5 tells us to judge no one after the flesh and further, to know one another by the Spirit. You can always determine your level of maturity in this by your response to people. If you are not responding well to people, you need to get refreshed in the presence of the Lord. Renew your purpose and recommit yourself to the will of God. Then you will find your focus in the right place, on God, so that you can see as He sees and respond as He responds.

Follow Through

It seems basic, but I cannot begin to tell you how important follow through is in outreach ministry. As Christians, what do we have except our word? When everything is stripped away—your beautiful clothes, knowledge of the Scripture, and eloquent prayer—the only thing left is your word.

People can be very cynical about Christians. They are looking for anything that will discount everything you say or do. Saying one thing and doing another is "numero uno" (number one) in the excuse book of why people say they do not want any part of religion. Christianity is not about religion; it's about relationship! It's about our relationship first and foremost to God, and then to everyone around us. Always do what you say you are going to do, even if the final outcome is not what you intended.

People in despair almost always have issues of mistrust. Many times they have been hurt by people since their childhood. When you show up, they are thinking, *So why should you be any different?* It means the world to people that you remember to do what you said you are going to do.

Whenever I am ministering somewhere, invariably I will promise to gather information or do something for someone. Do you know that the next time I see them, the first thing they ask is, "Did you...?" Answering *yes* always brings a smile that would light up the world. Developing trust with those you are ministering to is imperative. Let your yes be yes and your no be no. Make sure to follow up, and if you are not going to be able to get the information back to the person who asked the question, make sure someone else can. And acknowledge to the individual that someone else might follow up.

Guard Against Discouragement

Sometimes laboring in the field day in and day out, seeing no real change in the lives of those being touched, can cause us to feel discouraged or even make us want to quit. Don't do it. Sit back and realize that everything you are doing is having an impact, whether you see the fruit or not. Paul told us that there is a possibility that we will grow weary, or get discouraged while trying to do well. In Galatians 6:9 he charges us not to allow ourselves to grow weary in doing good for in due season we will reap. Paul also told us in 1 Corinthians 3:7 that, "Some plant, some water, but God gives the increase" (paraphrased).

Planting takes place when we sow the Word into the hearts of people. As we minister to those in need, we give them a scripture verse that will help them or simply share the Word of God. As we speak God's Word to them, it is like a seed being planted in their hearts. Jesus taught us about the parable of the sower, and in Matthew, Mark, and Luke's accounts, we see clearly that the Word of God is seed, and when the seed is sown into the hearts of those who hear, it will bear fruit. Each account speaks of the condition of the heart when the seed is sown, but it is not for us to determine the condition of the soil of anyone's heart except our own. If the soil of someone's heart is not ready to receive, then God will send another laborer along the path to declare the Word to them. The person who heard the Word before, but whose heart was not immediately ready to hear it, will remember the Word, and it will be watered. If the soil is not ready for harvest, the watering will continue until the individual is ready to respond to the Word. Only God can know when the harvest will come, and it is God alone who gives the increase.

What happens most often as we minister to others is that we are planting and watering, both equally important to the plan of God.

Without them nothing would transpire in the lives of people. Every once in a while, we will get to see the increase. When I speak of this, I'm not talking about leading people to the Lord, I'm speaking of seeing them later and hearing their great testimonies of how Jesus changed their lives. Those situations will come occasionally, and when we hear them, we are encouraged to continue our efforts to win the lost.

Never forget, your labor of love is not in vain (1 Corinthians 15:58). Remember always that God is at work in them both to will and to do for His good pleasure (Philippians 2:13). His Word that you have sown in their hearts will not return void (Isaiah 55:11); it will prosper in the thing for which God sent it. He watches over His Word to perform it in their lives. This is why some sow, then the Word is watered until a harvest comes. No one knows when the harvest will come. What is the harvest? Change in the life of the one who received the Word.

Discouragement is a powerful thing, and I know in my heart that many fell by the wayside when it came. The enemy wants us to focus more on the work of what we are doing than on the harvest. He wants us to faint and fall away, to give up and quit. When we know for sure that our every word—or shall we say God's every Word spoken through our lips—is eternally affecting the lives of those who hear, we will never give up. We will never shut up! We will never sit down!

Oh, God, give us a glimpse of our heavenly reward (people!), so we will be spurred on in our desire to reach out and bless them all the more.

Stay Under Cover

When I use the words "under cover," I'm speaking about staying submitted under the authority God has established for the ministry. God's order brings a blessing! There are no Lone Rangers in the kingdom of God. Every work that is established has someone at the helm directing the path. Usually this person has a vision or desire given by God to do something for His kingdom. Staying under cover means I stay under the covering of the authority that God has placed over me. When I walk in submission to those in authority, I walk in unity. When I stay in right alignment with my covering, I walk in peace.

We will never do anything great for God until we understand God's authority and how He delegates authority to men/women. Until we do, we will fight authority and refuse to submit every time a disagreement arises. In order to clearly understand God's order, we must accept that we are part of a kingdom, the kingdom of God. A kingdom is not a democracy where people can do and say whatever they want. A kingdom has a ruler, and the ruler is the king. The king decrees the way things will be done, and those who belong to the kingdom adhere to the decrees of the king. You can see where I am going here, since Jesus is the King, and we are a part of His kingdom.

Jesus prayed regarding unity in John 17, asking the Father that we would be one with Him as He is one with the Father. He knew the importance of unity if we are going to accomplish the work of the gospel in the earth. And we see in Psalm 133 that where there is unity, God gives a blessing. So walking together in unity, willingly submitting ourselves to God's Word and to those whom God has placed in authority over us, will bring a blessing to both our ministry and our personal lives.

Outreach ministry requires a group of individuals called to a single purpose who come together to minister to those in need within a certain area. There will always be a person within the group who is called and anointed by God to lead the group. This person will receive information from God by way of vision, dreams, desires, or passion to reach a certain group of people with the gospel. Then as he/she communicates the vision, people with the same passion will come alongside of him/her to help fulfill the vision.

To walk in true unity, we must have singleness of heart and mind. And to stay safe, we must obey the authority over us. If we do not acknowledge the authority and stay within the realm of influence we have been given, we could get hurt or hurt the plan of God because of our disobedience.

One of the greatest issues I see wherever I go is the issue of submission. It seems there are always people looking to promote themselves and be seen by those in authority to gain some advantage. I have learned over the years that there's one way the enemy always attacks. His first tactic is to divide. Jesus said a house divided against itself will not stand. Conversely, a house united will not fall. Unity is paramount in ministry. When I learned that my covering of authority would bring peace to my life and a blessing to my future, I decided to walk in unity with all people, because walking in peace is crucial. Let's face it, submission doesn't even come into play until a disagreement takes place. If everyone is happy and walking in agreement toward the same things, there is no need to submit. It's when disagreement comes that those who are under the authority of another must yield themselves to the decisions of the authority.

I was invited to go to India on a mission trip back in 2001. I was so excited! I had prayed for several years about going, and now the dream was finally becoming a reality. I remember arriving at the airport where the majority of the team was to meet. Right from the beginning, a married couple on the team started trying to take control over the head of the team. When I realized what was going on, I started to pray, asking God to intervene in their hearts so that division would not come to the team. Upon our arrival in Hyderabad, things got worse. Not only did the couple continue to exert control over the team leader, but there was complete disunity among the advance teams for the ministries that were doing the crusades in India. The tension was so high that it put a great amount of pressure on everyone. At one point, I was even asked to leave the team with this couple and go to a different location. I declined the offer and refused to do anything other than bless those whose authority God sent me under. The team was eventually split because of dissention among the members. It was so sad, because God had great plans for this team that the team allowed the enemy to divide. Who knows today what God would have done through the team if we had stayed together? One thing is for sure: those who continued on with the team God had established were blessed and fulfilled in every way. The members who split from the team ended up putting themselves in danger and becoming sick before the end of the trip. You see, we still had to meet up again to return home. When we did, the couple told us how they had rented a car to take them into a part of the city where there were many poor people. They wanted to show the Jesus Film and help people get saved. When they started showing the film, a mob of angry

Muslims tried to attack them. Thank God, they escaped unharmed. In addition, they were very ill on the trip home, because they had become dehydrated. Both of these situations would have been avoided if they had remained under the cover of the authority on the team. Our team leader had traveled to India many times and knew the city where we stayed, as well as the spiritual climate and need for nourishment. When this couple split from the team, they went out without the knowledge and wisdom necessary to live safely in a third world nation.

Why do these things happen when we try to do something good for God and His people? We cross the line, so to speak, in exerting our own knowledge or experience over the person God has put in authority, choosing to do what we want to do rather than obeying the authority over us.

Let's look at the account of Rahab and see what happened to her as she followed the instructions of those in God's authority. In the book of Joshua chapters 2 and 6, we see Joshua sending spies out to Jericho to determine if the Israelites could take the city and its inhabitants. When the spies arrived, they were taken in by Rahab. The king of Jericho sent to Rahab and asked her to bring out the spies, but she hid them and then sent them out of the city after the king's army had left the city thinking they were pursuing the spies. Before Joshua's men left, she acknowledged her belief in their God and said that she knew the Lord had given them the city of Jericho. The spies replied, telling her to stay quiet regarding their plans, and if she did they would deal kindly with her. The spies instructed her to put a scarlet cord on her window so that when the Israelites attacked the city, if she stayed inside her home with the scarlet cord on the window, and she or any of her family were harmed, her blood would be on the hands of the army of God. Conversely, if she left her home or did not put the scarlet cord on the window and harm came to her or her family, then her blood was on her own hand.

Rahab had to obey the commands of the spies in order to save herself and her family. The scarlet cord was a boundary she would not cross. In fact, in Joshua 2:18–21, the Scripture actually uses the wording "this line of scarlet." The cord was a line that could not be crossed. It was not only a promise for the future but also a decree that Rahab had to obey if she and her family were to be spared. Her obedience to the instruction saved her life and brought her into the future God had planned for her. The same is true of our obedience to God and those in authority. It will keep us safe and bring us into our God given destiny.

Chapter 7

OUT OF THE DARKNESS

This book was written from a heart that desperately desires for each person to recognize his or her worth, reach his or her full potential in Christ, and then return to the mire to help bring those left behind into the fullness of Christ. My heart burns with passion to reach the lost and dying, the hopeless and empty. I pray that reading this book has ignited your heart with the same passion to reach out and give people the only answer that can ultimately change their lives. The answer is Jesus.

Look for opportunities—there are people in need all around you. At every turn an invaluable human soul waits to hear the message of life in Christ. Remember, you are the messenger, the witness. Step across the invisible barrier of fear, and reach out to those in need with a message of hope. Be a person who helps restore hope in the hearts of those who are lost. Minister life to those who are dying! Go forth to those who are in darkness, show yourself! Then lead them out of the kingdom of darkness, and bring them into the glorious light of Jesus Christ! All of the power of heaven is backing you up. What are you waiting for?

ENDNOTES

1. The Harris Poll #90, "The Religious and other Beliefs of Americans 2005," December 14, 2005, www.harrisinteractive. com/harris_poll/index.asp?PID=618 © 2005.
2. The Barna Group, "Church Attendance," National Survey 2005, www.barna.org/flexpage.aspx?page=topic&topic=10.

Printed in the United States
78783LV00004B/280-306